The Retired

Landlord

By Cody Krell

TABLE OF CONTENT

Introduction 3
Chapter 1 Real Estate Management 11
Chapter 2 Real Estate Investing Basics 50
Chapter 3 Single Family homes vs. Condo 73
Chapter 4 Residential Multi-Family Property 80
Chapter 5 Large Apartment Complexes 87
Chapter 6 Finding an Agent 106
Chapter 7 Insurance 112
Chapter 8 Tax Benefits 125
Conclusion 138

Introduction

Real estate is primarily a business and not a profession.

A profession is a disciplined unit of individuals who adhere strictly to ethical standards. This individual tends to possess specialized knowledge and skills that have been derived from research, education, and training at a high level to protect the interest of the public; whereas a business is an organization entity engaged in a commercial or industrial enterprise for the benefit of profit.

Unlike a profession that requires skilled and knowledgeable individuals, a business doesn't. Instead what is needed is his/her 'interest.' However welcoming this sounds, the success, and failure of this venture which results in either a reward or loss is to be enjoyed alone, unlike a profession whose reward is shared with others., be it profit or loss.

With real estate being a business or a profession, it has no connection with the business ethics governing it.

Divisions of the business

Real estate is principally divided into three units; which are investment, operation, and agency. These units differ from each other according to the goals of the person engaging in them and the methods of practice employed to gain profit. To conduct business in the first two divisions of real estate (Investment or operation), 'capital' is needed. However, for the agency division, the most important capital required is the 'goodwill of its customers' which can be managed, increased and made very valuable.

Investment is the engagement of capital in the ownership of real estate.

The Retired Landlord

Operation is the employment of capital in the development, renting, leasing, and management of real estate.

Agency is an intermediary (representative) dealing in or with real estate on behalf of others.

Investment in real estate is generally for:

a. Generating income or profit

b. To hold for resale in expectancy of an increase in cost.

Investment for income can be derived from

I. Rental fees, or

II. The obtaining of income through others upon cash lent on the security of real property.

Real estate operations can be carried on;

a. For the sale and purchase of land

b. For building purpose

c. For mortgage purpose

The sales and purchase of land is a branch of operation that concerns itself with land dealings either to be sold and bought for profit and loss purpose. It can be divided into two;

i. Speculation purpose which involves an initial purchase of land to sell later to yield profit, which is more of a short-term investment.

ii. Developmental purpose which usually is a long-term investment that involves buying wholesale, developing them, marketing them and re-selling them in small units.

This part of real estate that concerns itself in development can be sub-divided into;

a. Speculative building which consists of building structures for the sole purpose of selling.

b. Investment building which is composed of erecting structures for personal dwelling or rental purpose.

The form of operation concerned with lending of money on real estate security is divided into 'Permanent' and 'temporary' loans.

Permanent loans are sums of money lent upon mortgages at modern-day interest price, the safety being deemed with the aid of the lender sufficient to find the money for an adequate margin between the amount of the mortgage and the actual cost of the property, the sum being loaned for an exact time.

Temporary loans are loans lent for property investment, to aid construction and maintenance. This loan is remitted after repairs, development or reconstruction has been completed. Due to the high risk of operation and the necessity of lender's supervision, there is an increased interest rate in compensation over and above the value of the loan. For this reason, it is to the borrowers' interest that the loan is made permanent rather than temporary.

Agency is the branch of real estate business that interests the attention of quite some persons concerned with the business. It is divided into 'brokerage' and 'management.'

A broker is a licensed professional that negotiates transactions between principals for compensation, without having title to the property.

Brokerage has two divisions, a 'sale' broker and a 'loan' broker depending on the business type that interests the broker.

The sale broker is a broker in the business of selling and exchanging real property, while a loan broker is one who devotes his/her attention to obtaining loans for real property security.

Management, the other branch of agency is concerned with the derivation of income and upkeep for real estate structures. In addition to this, it lowers expenses and the care in making expenditures.

Real estate is a kind of property. Property is the right to ownership. Real property is the legal right of possession consisting of land and building.

While we talk about real property, we use the phrases of their technical legal sense. While we speak of real estate as a commodity and business, it embraces the various components of the business which draws the interest of those who comply with it as a vocation, and consists of interest which lawfully cannot be considered real property, as an example, leases, mortgages, and so forth.

Chapter 1
Real Estate Management

Real estate management was forged around 1930's within the United States, during the times of high-quality depression after creditors reclaim on lots of mortgages, they found that the control of these houses, well completed. The cracking recession occurrence between the year 2007 and year 2009, once more intensified the call for professionally accomplished managers. These financial crises – integrated with an addition in absentee's possession of real estate, ownership by investment agencies through association, real estate investment trusts, and additional social process – have all enhanced the call for real estate management/control and further indicates its reputation as a cost-added line of work.

Real estate management is the governance of operation, advertising, maintenance, and financial supervision of real estate property to meet up with the owner of the property targets. It is a business service fashioned professionally, and as such, requires the managers work hand-in-hand with the owners of the properties they manage, not excluding the tenants and citizens living within those properties.

Real estate management is a very complicated commercial enterprise to handle as it requires usage of the contemporary era of growth working efficiency, increasing income streams, and revealing property gross performance. Managers must provide multifaceted fiscal reviews to owners of the property, diversify emergency approaches to defend people and properties, obey and comply with effective governmental policies, understand new-sprung hire provisions and phrases, and realize how to function properties in an environmentally sustainable and profit-making manner.

The Primary Focus Of A Real Estate Manager.

The responsibility of a real estate manager is enveloped under five (5) points:

1. Control of the physical belongings (property) – upkeep, inspections, operations, capital

Enhancements, sustainability.

2. Human resource control – dealing with the main folks that maintain and assist the properties operations.

3. Economic control – budgeting, accounting, financial and funding analysis, leverage, financing

4. Advertising and marketing and leasing – marketing plans and method, advertising and advertising and preparing the

gap for rent, showing the belongings, negotiating rentals, organizing rents.

5. Legal and risk control – insurance coverage, emergency planning, government rules, contracts, leases.

The work achieved employing real estate managers varies substantially depending on the position they hold, the type of agency or business enterprise they work for, and the sort of real estate property they control.

Positions in Real Estate Management

- Real Estate Manager

Real Estate Managers offers job possibilities at various ranges – ranging from front-line site handler to business enterprise executives. Also, a collection of personnel positions – accounting, advertising, leasing, Maintenance, human resources – assist overall real estate management obligations.

Specific real estate management jobs commonly fall into These broad classes:

- Site Manager

- Property Manager

- Regional Manager

- Property Manager

- Control Company Government

It is crucial to comprehend that the duties Related to those positions frequently overlap. At the Property level, there regularly are many similarities between obligations of the site manager and those of the Property supervisor. On the property or portfolio level, Parallels can be visible between the responsibilities of the Manager (local/regional) and those of the property supervisor/manager. The line of work titles and obligation will vary substantially depending on the kind of Organization and the type of properties that are being managed.

- Site Manager

A site supervisor is chargeable for the everyday operations of a single property. The appellation 'site manager' is chiefly drawn to 'managers of private possession,' alongside apartment and rental initiatives and owners' institutions. Site managers responsible for multifamily residential properties can be ascribed as on-site managers or, if they live in residencies they manage, they will be called resident managers. The site manager/supervisor for an office construction may have the title of building manager/supervisor. Less commonplace are site managers for retail properties.

The site manager bureaucracy a crucial link between properties tenants and residents and the properties manager, charged with duty for regular operations, the site manager is answerable for:

i. Preservation of the physical plant, ensuring that the properties are well maintained, and automatically examining the grounds and system to decide if repairs or renovation are required.

ii. Managing technical operations, such as mechanical and electrical systems.

iii. Advertising and leasing the property, displaying vacant space, negotiating and imposing the terms of rental or lease agreements.

iv. Tenant and resident members of the family, such as handling requests for maintenance and resolving complaints. For this purpose, strong communiqué and people skills are required to carry out successfully as a site manager/supervisor.

v. Collection of rents and keeping correct records of properties state, including income and expenditure, which allows the property manager to chart the economic performance of the possession.

vi. Supervising site workers, which mostly includes maintenance personnel and leasing agents, as well as contractors who may be performing a collection of services on the property.

- Property Manager

The title 'property manager' is typically associated with a single significant property or numerous properties. The position of a property manager for residential properties is commonly supervisory with oversight of multiple features, each having its site manager. The property manager for business homes, however, typically will be liable for a single large building or more than one houses where there are no site managers. In this situation, daily management is handled straightaway by the property manager with the support of an administrative assistant and other worker.

The property manager plays the role of a liaison between the property proprietor or proprietor's agent and site personnel. The property manager has direct responsibility for the tangible property, which the property represents, and specializes in handling the physical property– overseeing daily services of site managers, other site workers and work contracted out if any – and the monetary control of the property. The activities of the business precede a control plan, which the property manager has designed and the owner has accredited. This plan governs all elements of the physical plant, financial operation, tenant members of the family, marketplace positioning, and community image building. Of maximum significance, property/property managers are forthwith chargeable for keeping and creating value in homes; which is achieved by enhancing the net earnings of a property.

The center of a real estate property manager is on the property itself as funding, and selections made by property managers are those who impact on a properties financial overall performance. In lots of instances, the property manager is the consultant of the owner and chargeable for choosing a third-party control company and monitoring the overall performance of that agency. In all cases, the stress of 'property control' is on activities that will add worth to every property beneath management and the portfolio of properties as a whole, operational function, overall performance goals. The caretaker roles are committed to the 'property and site managers.'

- Regional Manager

A regional manager supervises property overall performance, examining revenues from the portfolio and studying costs to ensure a profitable activity. In many instances, responsibility for distinguishing and perusing predominant capital expenditure applications or re-positioning properties to ensure highest and top-grade use rests with the regional/ local manager. More routinely, regional managers make sure that the working and capital budgets for every property are well organized, valid and accepted and that month-to-month operating statements prepared for submission to the owner represents client objectives.

Regardless of the kind of property, the regional manager has the supervisory duty over the properties/ property managers of every property, in the portfolio in addition to the accountability for the property themselves. Because of this, recruitment, grooming, improvement, and supervision of property managers are vital obligations. On a regular base, regional managers will go to the properties in their portfolios, which could entail significant travel when properties are broadly spread. These site visits are essential to monitoring belongings performance, auditing operational and financial sports, carrying out marketplace analyses, main the properties management group, and making marketing and rental rate recommendations.

- Management Company Executive

A management company executive's proximity of concentration is often stretched towards operations of the real estate management agency/ company. The management company executives' obligations range extensively from company to enterprise relying upon its size, problems and opportunities, ability and skills of the management team, and the executive ownership role in the agency/ company.

The company executive, usually the chief executive officer, is, primarily an entrepreneur, who is always the primary manufacturer of new business establishment for the organization. It is also the job of the company executives to modify monetary outcomes of the commercial enterprise operation through efficient, strategic control of its opportunities and resources.

Tremendous time is spent making plans for the organization's service, growing and supervising the real estate management group, organizing and enforcing company regulations and procedures, developing and keeping an era platform and infrastructure, executing a possible organizational structure, and growing the business organization.

Properties that require management

The form of properties being managed has an immediate effect on the character of a real estate manager's work. There are numerous types of property, each having its peculiarities and putting precise demands on the supervisor or manager of that real estate.

From perspectives, the varieties of properties that demand management are being classified into: ***Commercial Properties*** and ***Residential Properties***.

Even though there are numerous similarities between handling residential and industrial homes, distinct differences do exist. The apparent differences are the nature of the tenants, the period of the hire phrases, the complexity of 'hire' payments, and the hours of use.

Dealing with and leasing shopping facilities are more complicated than different types of property. Further to handling the property itself, the real estate supervisor also may be without delay liable for the ongoing increase and achievement of the retail tenants and their commercial enterprise firms.

Managers of shopping facilities should also provide a smooth and safe environment that appeal to customers and take part in advertising and marketing applications that target the demographics and psycho-graphics of the purchasing center's alternate place.

The term "commercial properties" in its broadest definition encompasses all real estate development that isn't always exclusively residential and refers to properties wherein a business activity takes location, and This consists of:

- Office homes

- Uniqueness workplace buildings, most considerably clinical office buildings

- Buying facilities, strip facilities, department stores, retail residences

- Research parks

- Warehouses - wherein space is being leased for storage of stock, extra substances, and so on

- Self-garage homes or mini-warehouses - which resemble rows of connected garages and are used by people and small businesses to store goods for themselves.

- Commercial properties- that may include varying from big single-consumer houses to incubator area for small Commercial enterprise start-ups.

Even though there are numerous similarities betwixt residential and commercial properties, distinct variations do exist. The plain varieties are the character of the tenants, the period of the rent terms, the complexity of lease payments, and the hours of use.

Managing and leasing shopping facilities usually are more complicated than other properties. In addition to managing the property type, the real estate manager also may be accountable for the ongoing growth and fulfillment of the retail tenants and their commercial businesses. Management determines the tenant blend, with a close watch towards selecting retailers who serve the shopping center's client base and complement the center's existing uses. Furthermore, managers of shopping centers need to offer elegant and secure surroundings that appeal to shoppers and take part in advertising and marketing applications that target the demographics and psycho-graphics of the shopping center's trade region.

The market for office building is complex and competitive, requiring a knowledgeable and responsive management approach. The owner of an office building mostly has more sophisticated maintenance responsibilities than the supervisor or manager of other property types. Managers of office structure are frequently confronted with the responsibility of imparting a healthy surrounding that will increase productiveness for the employees of the tenants whose business are administered in those place of work. The sort of businesses operated within the property determines all elements of the building's dealings, from amenities offered to ultimate building system performance. Emergency routines can be an extra workload for the owner of an office building due to the number of people concentrated in a vertical tower. Parking and movement of humans inside and outside the building construction are management worries, and the mechanical, safety, and energy conservation systems are incredibly technical. Clinical workplace homes constitute a niche marketplace within the office building section that requires extraordinary specialized management skillfulness.

'Industrial properties' have evolved from utilitarian production buildings to modern, master-planned commercial transformation. They vary extensively in characteristic and size and may include something from a 1,000-square-foot storage warehouse to an incubator building with many small start-up organizations to a multi-tenanted industrial park or distribution center encompassing hundreds of acres.

Industrial property managers offer an environment where corporations can either move or manufacture merchandise for clients, concerning product logistics; managers make contributions via imparting sophisticated business properties wherein tenants can move, stock, allot, and convey merchandise in a timely fashion to fulfill client desires on both domestic and international scale.

Residential properties are those wherein humans live, either as condominium tenants or as owners. Residential properties are defined using the kind of ownership, the sort of financing, and the varieties of tenants and residents.

The list of residential properties that demand management includes:

The Retired Landlord

- Apartments– conventionally financed rentals.

- Apartments–government-assisted and less costly housing, which incorporates suburban condominium residences in which the landlord receives all or a part of the hire charge from a governmental frame.

- Public housing – owned and managed with the aid of a nearby or state regulatory agency.

- Condominiums, cooperatives, owners' associations, and other common-interest modification.

- Rental single-family homes.

- Mobile home parks – in which citizens own their houses but hire the land and pay an access charge for utilities and ordinary areas.

- Single -room occupancy apartments.

- Student housing.

- Senior housing and housing for the aged – which vary from independent living to complete-scale assisted living.

- Military housing – owned and operated by the military directly or by private groups under contract with the military.

Rental housing ranges from huge apartment blocks in high-rise apartment buildings to a single-family home. Rental housing operates for 24 hours a day/seven days a week; should meet all of the wishes of residents' day-to-day lives. This non-stop occupancy tends to increase the request for maintenance and repair. Service demand is high. Because residents accurately expect where they live to be "home," even when they are renters, there may be an emotional investment in the real estate as well as a financial investment. Managers of residential properties make sure that residents are provided with clean, secure, and healthy surroundings that they could call home. With the aid of meeting those critical expectation, property managers not only impart to the nicely-being of the citizens but also to the community that surrounds the property. For this reason, residential property managers need to have strong people skills in addition to their administrative skills.

- Mixed-use properties:

A mixed-use property is one that consolidates multiple usages within a single project. Such residences might contain commercial and residential use in addition to entertainment and cultural use or industrial use. In metropolitan regions, mixed-use developments with residential units or commercial space on higher floors and ground-floors retail are very well-known, and more extensive combined-use planned communities are a growing trend.

With its definition, a mixed-use property is inherently more complicated to manage than a single -use property. This complexity may be similarly elevated when there are more than one ownership structures – for example, rental-owned residential units combined with investor-owned retail space.

Real Estate Investment

Real estate investment involves "the procurement, possession, management, apartment and sale of real estate for profit." development of realty property as part of a real property funding strategy is commonly considered to be a sub-forte of real estate investing referred to as real estate development. The Real estate is an property shape with restrained liquidity relative to different investments, it is also capital in depth (even though money can be earned through loan leverage) and is entirely coins flow established. If those elements are not well understood and controlled via the investor, the real property will become an unstable investment. The number one reason of investment failure for real estate is that the investor is going into poor coins drift for a period that is not sustainable, regularly forcing them to resell the property at a loss or move into insolvency. A comparable practice known as flipping is any other motive for failure because the nature of the investment is frequently related to brief period earnings with much less attempt.

Real estate markets, nearly in all countries are not as structured or efficient as other markets. Individual properties are specific to themselves and not directly exchangeable, which offers a significant contest to an investor in quest of evaluating costs and funding opportunities. For this reason, locating properties for investment can contain enormous work and competition among investors to purchase individual properties may be extraordinarily variable relying on the knowledge of availability. Information imbalance is common in real estate markets, and this increases the risk in transactions. However, it also presents many possibilities for traders to acquire properties at bargained charges. Real estate marketers typically use different estimation techniques to determine the value of properties before purchase.

Well-known sources of investment properties comprise of:

- Market listings (using Multiple Listing Service or Marketing Information Exchange)
- Real estate agents and brokers
- Banks
- Government entities or agencies
- Public auction (foreclosure auctions, estate sales, etc.)
- Private sales (transactions for sale by owner, i.e., For sale by owner)
- Real estate wholesalers and investors (flipping)

Once an investment property/business whereabouts has been discovered and explored due diligence (research and confirmation of the situation and status of the property) completed, the investor will have to talk terms with the vendor/ seller, then execute an agreement for sale.

Most investors/buyers hire real estate marketers and real property lawyers/attorneys to help with the purchase process, as it could be pretty complicated and improperly performed. Transactions can be costly. In the course of the acquisition of a property, an investor will typically make a formal offer to buy including payment of "earnest money" to the vendor/seller at the beginning of the negotiation to reserve investor's rights to complete the transaction if the price and terms are agreeable.

This earnest cash may or may not be refundable, and is considered to be a signal of the seriousness of the investor's intention for acquisition. The terms of the offer may include some of the contingencies which permit the investor time to complete due diligence, look into the properties and acquire financing among different necessities prior to final purchase or acquisition.

During this contingency period, the investor commonly has the right to rescind the offer without a penalty and gain money back of earnest money deposits. As soon as contingencies have expired, rescinding the offer will typically require forfeiture of the earnest money deposits and may involve other penalties as well.

Real estate properties are typically very highly-priced in assessment to different available investment instruments (which includes stocks or bonds). It is rare for a real estate investors/buyers to pay the whole amount of the acquisition fee of property in cash. Commonly, a big part of the acquisition charge is presumably financed employing the use of some financial tool or debt, including a loan collateralized by the property.

The quantity of the purchase price funded through debt is called leverage. The amount financed using the investor's capital, through cash or other property transfers, is referred to as equity. The ratio of leverage to global appraised price (often referred to as "LTV," or loan to value for a conventional mortgage) is one mathematical measure of the risk an investor is taking through the use of leverage to finance the acquisition of property.

Investors are usually looking for how to decrease their equity requirements and increase their leverage, to maximize their return on investment (ROI). Lenders and exceptional economic establishments typically have minimum equity requirements for real estate investments they are requested to finance, generally on the order of 20% of appraised value. Investors/buyers looking for low equity requirements may additionally discover other trade financing arrangements as a part of the acquisition of properties.

If the property calls for huge repairs, conventional creditors like banks will often not lend on a property, and the investor/buyer can be required to borrow from a private lender utilizing a short-term bridge loan like a hard cash loan from a hard money lender. Hard money loans are short-term loans wherein the lender charges a significant fee due to the higher risk it attracts to itself. Hard money loans are regularly at a much decrease loan-to-value ratio than conventional mortgages.

Some real estate investment groups, such as Real Estate Investment Trusts (REITs) and some pension funds and hedge funds, have sufficient capital reserves and investment techniques to permit a 100% equity in the properties that they buy, this minimizes the risk which comes from leverage but additionally limits potential ROI.

Using 'leverage' the procurement of an investment property and required periodic payments to service the debt creates an ongoing (and occasionally substantial) negative cash flow starting from the time of purchase, which is sometimes known as the carrying cost of the investment.

To achieve success, real estate traders/investors ought to manage their income from the property to create enough profits from the property to minimize or possibly offset the carry costs.

With President Obama's signing of the JOBS Act in April 2012, there has been an easing on the funding request. A recent method of raising equity in smaller quantities is through real estate crowd funding that pools authorized and non-authorized investor/buyers together in a special purpose vehicle needed for the purchase. "Fundrise" happens to be the first business enterprise to crowd fund a real estate investment in the U.S.

Real estate investment has appeared quite popular in recent years due to increasing values in property and the decreasing rates of interest.

Investing Basics

If you are new to investing, the query you're probably asking yourself is: "what must I do first?"

It is not always a straightforward query to answer for a person who is merely starting to manage his/her portfolio. There are numerous options available, with hardly subtle difference among a few selections. Importantly, you do not need your first investment to be a losing one.

So, how do you begin?

It does not matter if you are a brand new investor beginning with a small portfolio or a person who is taking on their investments for the first real time, the steps are equal. So take the most important first step.

Getting Started as an Investor!

- **Create a Plan**

Investing is a longtime project that continuously evolves. As is the case with every project, success starts with a well-considered idea/ concept. A map of what you need to accomplish and the steps to take to get there is required. You never recognize all the requirement while you start a task, but it is a must you have an idea of what you need to find out as you advance.

Of course, every massive project encounters sudden twists and turns. Investing is indeed no different; if anything, it meets even greater twists and turns. But, when you have a good plan mapped out, you'll have a framework to fall back on while the unexpected eventually happens.

What ought to be to your plan?

When developing your plan, you need to concentrate on the bigger picture and not the information. Investing can get complicated quickly, so it's miles essential to keep things at this stage very simple.

Priorities your plan needs to cover;

a. Financial Desires

Are you looking to build wealth through the years, preserve capital, pay for a particular cost (e.g., college for your kids), or is there a few different aims? Preferably, is there more than one goal that you hope to fulfill? Many human beings have a couple of purposes. If that describes you, all you need do is pen down those desires and the number of years you need to attain each goal.

b. Risk Tolerance

What is your ability to cope with losses? Are you capable of handling damages resulting from a bear market? Or, how accurately might you be able to sleep at night time if one or more of your investments experienced a massive swing in price? You may seem to answer these questions based on your emotions. However, the case, your financial state of affairs and dreams are crucial factors.

c. Personal Involvement

How active do you want to be? Some human beings enjoy the activity of selecting, analyzing and tracking individual securities. Others prefer a gentle approach, such as making an investment in a mutual fund or letting a financial planner be in charge of the decisions. Many incorporate a collection of both. The answer to this question narrows down to how involved you choose to be physically and whether you have time to supervise your investments actively.

Factors to be considered before investing in real estate:

- Place

- The approach of financing the purchase of the property

- Before tax coins waft

- After-tax coins waft

- Vacancy charge for apartment belongings

- Gain or loss for tax purposes

- Control troubles

Areas to consider for investment;

- Do it in stock wherein the gains can be significant, not in corporate bonds.

- You are better off buying a high-quality bond issue.

- Purchase stocks when they are undervalued and hold for the long term.

The Retired Landlord

- Do not invest in a tax shelter unless it appears to be a good investment.

- Do not spend much on precious metals because of volatility.

- Buy into a mutual fund that shows a consistent long-term performance (e.g., five or ten year period) and did well in both good and bad markets. A mutual fund may show great performance only in one year because of luck, unusual circumstances, or the risky stocks bought shot up.

- Buy real estate in an excellent location and hold for 5-7 years.

Warning: Avoid selling short, buying options, and investing in commodities because these are short-term, risky investment strategies, and if you are wrong on timing and market direction, you may suffer significant losses.

The concepts of letting your money make you money

Creating and maintaining wealth evolves from saving. Unfortunately, there is no shortcut here. The folks who maxed out their account in 2000 and 2001 to make investments in the stock market paid a lousy fee for seeking to go the easy way. The concept of letting your money create wealth for you is the conventional example of the tortoise and the hare. To get rich, it is not necessary to make a onetime "killing." a much advisable method to making a living is to apply the knowledge of compound interest.

One dollar invested for 20 years at 4% is equal to $10.96(double your money), at 6% your money triples to $3.20, at 10% it will increase to $6.72, and at 14% your initial investment impressively yields $13.74. No need to make a killing. All that is needed is endurance and a sound investment scheme.

Commercial real estate opportunities offer rates of return that bring forth big payoffs through the power of compound interest. The trick to have in mind here is that higher profits work hand-in-hand with higher risk. While you receive an offer to have a high return with less risk, watch your pockets and run for cover.

Nevertheless, opportunities with superior returns relative to the risk abound in today's commercial real estate market, and this condition is likely to hold for some time.

Chapter 2
Real Estate Investing Basics

- ***Rental property investing***

Real estate investment covers a much broader spectrum of investment vehicles than an impressive number of people realize. This spectrum ranges from (1)- The passive 'Short-term' investment approach of buying real estate-related stocks on a public exchange, i.e. investing in Real Estate Investment Trusts (REITs) or maybe investing in deals and offers through a real estate platform, e.g., crowdfunding, to (2)- The 'Long-term' investment approach of buying individual residences at once — either to resell them for profit or to rent them out for ongoing benefits.

Among the benefit of investing in a rental is that it has the opportunity to offer two types of return. Firstly, it offers appreciation over longer term, if the property price-value increases over time and because of upgrades made with the aid of the owner, and as the owner increase the equity in the property by paying down the loan/mortgage.

Secondly, the owner can also realize an ongoing return in the investment, I.e., in the form of positive cash-flow - earned by rentals of property to tenants for monthly basis payments that surpass the owner's overall monthly expenses to maintain the property.

If an investor can;

1. Gain attractive financing to secure a property on rent and produces positive cash-flow in an appreciating market, and

2. Be willing to take on the obligation of managing the property (or working with a property management agency) — then investing in rental property can be seen as a feasible real estate investment method. Just as with any investment,

it is essential to understand that investing in rental property contains the risk of losing and a 'no' guarantees of return.

How to Invest in Rental Real Estate

Investing in rental real estate can provide you with a steady stream of cash that becomes profit after a property is fully paid for. However, attaining to such extent is risky and calls for much more work than it appears to do. Making an investment in real estate would require you to select a fantastic property. After that, maintaining such property, dealing with its tenants indefinitely or until you are making enough profits, to getting yourself a manager.

To invest in a rental real estate, the steps to follow has been classified into three parts:

- **Part 1- *Assess your ability to invest.***

For you to be certain about your investment ability, there are things expected of you, among those things are:

1. *Assess your ability to manage the property.*

Being a landlord is neither a passive income nor a part-time job. You will have to perform many responsibilities when it comes to property management. This includes choosing and communicating with tenants, ensuring property repairs when necessary and having to deal with a large variety of daily problem. Should in case you don't have time to manage the property yourself, you would have to employ a competent property agency. However, this may be prohibitively expensive at first.

2. Seek a buy-to-let Mortgage.

To be able to rent out a property, plainly you will have to buy it first. This can be accomplished with a buy to let loan/mortgage, which is evaluated differently than an owner-occupied loanee/mortgage. The bank will consider the rental income and expense capability of the property against the owner's potential to pay for it.

3. Make sure you have financial reserves.

Owning a rental property may warrant unexpected problems. Your tenant can lose their job and therefore unable to meet-up (pay) the rent. You have to have sufficient cash in the bank to get you through months with no money coming in. Some owners solely depend on the rent to pay off their mortgage. If you fall into that category, then-then you are strongly advised not to purchase until you have a six-month reserve that you can depend on.

Be reminded about the need to pay for tax on the property, not forgetting maintenance fee on the property. Furthermore, you are to prepare for unexpected expenses which can range from less expensive to very expensive, depending on the type.

4. *Invest for the long term.*

Do not opt to buy real estate as an investment unless you've got more than the ten-year horizon. Housing bubbles seem to come every 10 to 15 years, and everybody desires a piece of the action. A significant amount of people never gets the chance to back-out in time and therefore get financially hurt. Intelligent investors are not always carried-away by greed and short-term returns. They purchase homes that make significance profit as a rental, not as quick opportunity to make money.

5. Locating Partners.

Investing with a partner or partners can offer some benefits. Partners can pool resources and skills among themselves, taking into account extra investment achievement. But, you may need to find companions that are truthful and easygoing to work with. Ideally, you should get a companion with a talent set complementary to yours.

As an instance, if you excel at household improvements and maintenance, try locating a partner who is talented with crunching numbers. Set up your partnership with a working agreement that lays out duties, contributions, and the department of returns. Having a partner can provide you with the ability to qualify without difficulty for a mortgage.

- **Part 2- Locate a rental property**

To locate a rental property, you need to;

1. Find an ideal rental Market

Search for a local rental marketplace that is top notch and also accommodate excessive demand for rental homes. The tenant pool should consist of human beings who have made economic errors in the past and cannot qualify to buy. There may also be individuals who have lost their homes in foreclosures. The market should have experienced a price increase during the last year.

Ideally, you need to make investments someplace near home which you are already familiar with. Otherwise, you may need to do in-depth research.

2. Start with one, small property.

Even if you have the money, you should not soar into real estate investing with a big or complex property. Big properties like shopping facilities or condominiums can also have extra necessities or even need large down payments. As a substitute, begin with a single-family home that is within budget. This would let you get accustomed to being a landlord and the bookkeeping required of you.

Find properties via online searching for listings at websites like realtor.com, redfin.com, zillow.com, and trulia.com. You could additionally use a realtor who works with investors.

Colossal apartment units like 2 and 3-bedroom units require additional renovation than smaller units, and despite the fact that realtors describe these residences as, "bread and buffer units," they may be overwhelming, "nightmare" properties to first-time landlords.

Small rental units like studios, bachelors, and singles tend to rent to individuals that move around a lot and possess little furniture. Small rental units, though, "low key," will have lots of vacancies and it is crucial you expect this before you purchase the property.

3. Invest in commercial properties.

Commercial properties offer substantial potential returns than residential properties. However, finding and making an investment in them is always very difficult and is best executed by well experienced real property investors. If you want to purchase a commercial real estate, it is of great importance that you evaluate the property based on cost-price and potential returns from renters. And to be able to qualify for a loan, down payment of nothing less than 30% would be required.

4. Evaluate return potential

Your primary goal ought to be on your potential return on the property, which is the rent you acquire minus any expense. This is dependent on the prevailing rent in the area and the specific qualities of the house which allows you to charge more rent or less rent. Ask the property owner for financial information concerning the property, especially if they had been renting it out.

Also check out for the following:

- The loan price you will be paying.

- The current rent, rent charged for similar properties in the location, and any historical rent increases.

- The strength of the rent records. If a tenants move out, for how long does it remain vacant?

- Average property expenses

- Profits or losses for the property owner over few past years

- Your capacity to earn a return based totally on this records. Consider: rent - expenses= your return.

- Estimation of maintenance expenses.

5. Assess the property's location

The location is perhaps the essential feature of a rental home for renters. An excellent area of location can also allow you to fill the property without problems and even justify higher rental rates. Better tenants will are seeking out these properties and offer you with more dependable rent payments with fewer difficulties. Specifically, search for properties that are:

i. Close to good facilities.

ii. Located in low-crime regions.

iii. Convenient for shopping and facilities.

6. Make sure you get a good-deal

Search for the one's residences that are at, or near the bottom, and especially at homes marketed below their building cost. If cost price is low and interest fees are too, that collection makes buying perfect. Talk to a local real estate broker and hire an appraiser to determine the value of the property- either a good value or bad.

7. Make an offer

Work with your realtor or a selling agent to put in an offer after locating a fantastic property. Do not base your judgment emotionally, always buy a property that has a proper price tag. You may consent to walk away if you and the seller cannot come to a beneficial agreement.

8. Perform Due diligence

After your offer has been accepted, need to get your financing in order, at the same time you need to make sure that the property is in proper shape. Have a home inspector look for any issues with the property. To enable you to renegotiate the selling price. Ensure that the current owner did not merely cast off constructive repairs that will initiate a call for repairs when it becomes yours.

- ***Part 3- Finding Tenants***

In the quest of finding a tenant, there are some essential steps to note;

i. Obtain insurance.

ii. Determine appropriate rent for your property.

iii. Market your rental property.

iv. Screen applicants; some might have a lengthy criminal record.

v. Draft a rental agreement.

- ***Part 4- Maintaining Your Property***

Over the course of maintaining your property, it is vital for you to keep tabs on the tax levied on your property, learn some minor maintenance skill, develop relationships with industry professionals such as electricians, plumbers, and other tradesmen for you to get dependable work when the time comes for it. Also consulting a lawyer and accountant for your rental property is not a bad idea.

There are times you need to respond to tenants' need which may constitute a lot of repairs. You must learn to deal with tenants and their needs in a respectful and timely fashion, as it will alleviate the pain of incurring high vacancy expenses on your property.

Over the course of maintenance, there might be needful need to hire a property manager. Hiring a property manager can be very beneficial as it relieves the burden of landlord duties which includes the collection of rents, finding tenants for vacancy property, maintenance of property among other responsibilities. Property Managers comes handy when a landlord resides far away from his property, or he/she owns an impressive number of rental properties.

■ Wholesaling homes

Wholesaling is a term used in real estate business to explain the process of finding excellent real property deals and getting paid to convey them to real estate investors. It is much like a "finder's fee."

Wholesaling real estate is a short period investing method. Few people confuse this with fixing and flipping. However, there are differences. Wholesaling real property is useful if you need to get into real estate but don't have enough cash, but downfalls encompass confusion on its legality and complicated contracts.

Many humans suppose that turning into a real estate wholesaler is a clean way to starting a professional investment in real estate, but that is far from the truth. Only the people who are willing to work hard, and go through the procedure of turning into a professional at locating and buying the best financing homes, can be successful as a real property wholesaler.

Real estate wholesalers do enormous research to find out steeply discounted investment houses, then either buy them or location them beneath agreement and then quickly sell them or reassign the residences to another real estate investor.

What is illegal about Wholesaling?

Wholesaling real property is legal! However, it involves finding a distressed property which is followed by a proposal. The offer will be contingent on you marketing it to another investor. Once the investor purchases the property, a wholesale deal is complete.

There are various components to be aware of. Regulations and rules vary by states, so it is always useful to seek local real estate investment agency for recommendations. It is also beneficial to spend little money on consultations with a real estate attorney in your location because there are a lot of grey areas.

The essence of the debate on whether or not wholesaling is illegal revolves around the term "brokering."

Folks that argue that real property wholesaling is illegal claim it to be so due to the fact the wholesaler is performing as a "broker" inside the deal without being certified while those who defends wholesaling without a license say that wholesaling isn't always brokering, but signing a contract and then re-assigning that contract to another, and therefore the law is concerned with this example. Instead of selling a property, theirs is to promote the ownership of that real estate contract.

To further complicate things, there is the issue of "advertising and marketing" a property that you do not presently own. Most states also include "advertising and marketing a property" as brokering.

However placing a deal below contract, advertising and marketing the deal all over craigslist, and assigning that deal is a fast way to get fined by your state authorities and get a nice misdemeanor on your record!

How to wholesale?

How do you protect yourself from breaking the law while wholesaling? Here are a few tips that may be helpful.

1. Get a license

2. Find a Distressed property to Wholesale; This can be achieved through real estate wholesale and real estate investment groups, online real estate sites, and also you can make use of an assistant, mostly a property finder and realtors.

3. Make an offer and convince the owner to sell

4. Find a title company, contractor, and appraiser

5. Assess property's Renovation Needs

6. Find and Negotiate a deal with a buyer

7. 'Closing' on the Wholesale Property

■ Flipping

There are diverse of concepts regarding 'Flipping.'

When some people refer to "flipping houses," many are referring to the method of purchasing deeply distressed houses at auction, from foreclosure or financial institution sales at a deep discount, then quickly "flipping" (selling) that property to a homeowner without much in the way of renovations. Despite the fact that this type of residence flipping is popular and potentially lucrative, this not the kind of house flipping we're relating to right here.

That sort of "flipping" is based on little or quick income. Lamentably at the same time, this type of "flipping" process has given the real estate investing organization a bit of black eye. This kind of flipping is not only irresponsible, but yields less compared to the traditional way of purchasing, renovating and flip style of house flipping.

When you buy a distressed property, make no renovations, and quickly "flip it" to a buyer, you, in reality, don't add value to such a buyer. However when you buy a distressed property, renovate and sell it, you tend to add real value. And the real value begets even much more profit potential. This is the sort of house flipping that not presents bright living spaces for households and individuals but also helps to continue to bolster the emerging housing recovery.

Moreover, house flipping is typically referred to and occasionally confused with wholesaling. Wholesaling real estate is often referred to as "flipping" due to the fact a wholesaler "flips" a contract to a real estate investor who then does whatever pleases them with the property.

Real estate flipping can be referred as the purchase of property by real estate investor, generally at a lower fee, and the resale of same property at profit months down the road.

Can you be making cash doing this? Yes. Can you're making a whole lot of money doing this? Sure. But you can also lose the entirety you very own if you make an awful selection.

Contrary to what many people suppose, rapidly appreciating markets are not necessarily an essential component for house flipping success. House flipping, being a short-term fashion of real estate investing, is resistant to severe market fluctuations. And as a result, house flipping is most successful under any market conditions.

While thinking about it, house flipping is one of the least risky kinds of real estate investing there is. Inasmuch you purchase rightly, supervise well, stick to your price range and put a cease product on the property that proposes beauty and priced appropriately; you are sure to earn profit flipping houses.

Chapter 3
Single Family homes vs. Condo

Single-Family Home

The real property industry refers to single-family homes that stay on their own without having to share any partitions with home or building as detached houses. It is a single structure with its surrounding property, though it can differ regarding the planning, size, and vicinity.

Advantages:

— Independence is at a maximum.

— Cost price usually will increase over time, creating an investment for the owners of such property.

— Storage space permits for extra material possessions.

— Freedom to personalize the home to your taste.

Disadvantages

- Maintenance may be time-consuming and very costly.

- Cleaning can be stressful due to its prominent space.

- Cost price can be higher than other home types.

Condominium

A condominium often referred to as an attached apartment or condo is one unit of a large building. The difference between them is which you rent the former and purchase the latter.

Advantages:

- Maintenance is covered.

- Utility bills may be decreased due to the fact you might not be responsible for heat or water.

- Amenities, together with safety and fitness centers, can be included.

Disadvantages:

- Privacy is never assured.

- It might not have a designated garage.

- Space is quite limited.

Based on U.S. Census Bureau Statistics and a 2010 American community survey, about 60 to 79 percent of house owners in America opted for a detached house between 1949 and 2010. Detached housing offers distance among neighbors, a more significant experience of privacy and more floor space than attached housing.

The National Affiliation of Realtors reports that historical pricing for condominiums existing before now is less than the average price of single-family homes; people's way of life (lifestyle) has factored this. Geographical location also plays a function to this, as urban dwellers usually have greater access to condominiums. Both condos and single-circle of relatives' houses have their benefits and drawbacks.

The traditional possession of a detached home is known as "fee simple," Where you possess the building and its land. While someone purchases a condo, you only own the interior building space. However, the ownership of exterior walls, land and all common areas are shared amongst the proprietors. Proprietors of single-family homes can rent or lease the house as they see fit. Condo proprietors are subject to the regulations and rules laid down by the condominium development or home owner's association

The acquisition fee for a single-family home or condo varies depending on the size, amenities, condition and geographic area. The cost of maintaining a home also differs. Proprietors of single-family homes are responsible for the overall cost of all maintenance and repairs. Condo proprietors are individually accountable for upkeep and repairs within the condo but share the cost of maintenance for all common areas and other fees related to running the development. Rental proprietors typically pay for these expenses through a monthly fixed charge.

The best regulation of a single-family home has those set forth by state or governments. These usually need do with protection, zoning and noise issues. Condo owners need to adhere to the development's covenants, conditions and regulations document.

The policies outlined in many apartments CC&R document files are intolerant, limiting the colors you may paint your home, objects you may put in your yard and on occasion your landscaping selections. Single-family homes situated in gated communities can also have similar policies. However, they remain less restrictive.

Condos offer a unique lifestyle than single-family homes. Even though they lack privacy, in view that everyone within the building shares yards and common areas; they frequently have higher facilities than single-family homes. A number of the services rendered by condo developments include swimming pools, business facilities, and even golf courses. Life in a condominium apartment is more comfortable than single-family homes since all outdoor maintenance is sorted out by the development, unlike the single-family homes.

Appreciation and resale is another difference between the condo and single-family homes as the single-family homes tend to value more than a condo. The resale of condos mostly depends on the development's amenities. However, purchasing a condo is often subjected to based on lifestyle choice.

This is not law but based on how I run my company currently, I can save 17% of the total income from the rental and for the purpose of repairs and vacancy for my condo properties. While for my Single-family properties, I save 23% of the total rent for same purpose.

The Retired Landlord

For example: Supposedly the total rent for a condo apartment is 1200 per month, out which I decide to save 17% of that money which is equal to 204. So 1200 - 204 equals a balance of 996 which becomes my profit. Likewise, if the total rent for my Single Family on a monthly basis is 1200, I decide to save 276 which is approximately 23% of my rent while the balance of 924 becomes my profit.

I just wanted to show you that you do not necessarily have to save much for reserves when you own a condo investment property, condo gets a bad reputation in the investing game.

The danger of saving excessively for a reserve is the fact that you have falsely created a month-to-month condominium price that is quite high, and property values might crumble as a result of your reservation fee.

Cody Krell

Chapter 4
Residential Multi-Family Property

Multi-family residential

Multifamily residential (also called multi-dwelling unit or MDU) is a classification of housing where multiple detached housing units for residential dweller are contained within one building structure or various building structure inside one complex. Once in a while units in multifamily residential, residential buildings are condominiums, wherein the units are usually owned individually instead of being leased from a single rental building proprietor.

Types of Multi-family residential

1. Duplex/ two-flat

2. Triplex / three-flat

3. Quadplex or Four-flat

4. Semi-detached: usually a building consisting of two separate houses, side by side, each with its entrance.

5. Townhouse

6. Apartment building: a building with multiple apartments and floors.

7. Mixed use building: a building consisting of space which can be used for both commercial and residential use.

8. Apartment community: a collection of building sharing a common ground and amenities such as pools and parking areas. e.t.c.

House Hacking

House hacking is an exquisite real estate investment strategy when owning multi-family rental properties. House hacking is the scenario of living in one of the multiple units of your investment property as your primary place of dwelling, and feature renters residing on other units having to pay your mortgage and expenses costs.

House hacking can also occur in single-family homes while the investor lives on the same property, make improvements, and looks to resell the property within a short-term. Renting out a bedroom, basement, or additional part of your home can also be perceived as house hacking.

This is a robust approach for buyers trying to do a short restoration-and-turn, or for investors looking to shop for a proprietor-occupied multi-circle of relative property, such as a duplex, triplex or quadplex.

Why House Hack?

The principle behind hacking is that other people preferably renters pay for your housing expenses, thereby allowing you to concentrate on growing your real estate portfolio.

Benefits of House Hacking

1. Cash Flow

This is a significant benefits in house hacking rental properties—extra income amassed every month after all expenses have been settled. You could use your cash flow to either pay down your loan, or spend it investing in additional properties.

2. Financing

Investors develop the likeness for house hacking because it offers a method for financing a real estate deal. If you pick out to fund through an FHA mortgage, you may get a property for just 3.5% down. In other words, if you buy a $300,000 duplex, so you'll only need to put down $10,500. Remember that you must account for closing costs, however, when looking to lock a 30-yr fixed-rate mortgage, an FHA loan may be a fantastic option to get you started. Note there are many FHA mortgage pre-qualification, such as "owner occupancy" for 12 months. FHA loans are bounded by limits depending on your area of location.

3. Land lording

House hacking provides many first-time home buyers and real estate investors a valuable experience in being a landlord associated with low risk. This includes advertising your vacancy, tenant screening, tenant management, rental agreements and contracts apprehension, managing unanticipated housing issues and repairs, negotiating with contractors, and bookkeeping.

4. Lenders like Experience

If you seek for conventional financing in the future, traditional lending institutions—assume small, medium, and large banks—wish to see which you successfully own and managed rental properties in the past. Experience will enhance your opportunity of incurring large loans.

5. A starting point for New Real Estate Investors

Since you will be residing in your home as your primary house, all the advantages of proprietor occupancy will be at your fingertips. House hacking is a remarkable real estate investing strategy if you seek to take immediate action. You will not only have an incredible pulse on your property, but you will gain experience in expanding your real estate portfolio down the road. In the end, you would not be able to occupy every real estate investment as a number one residence and get to research through taking action.

Not all deals result in success. Be careful and do your homework while researching, financing, and acquiring real estate investments. There are always awful offers accessible, so make sure to spend the perfect time and energy in taking the proper steps. This could increase your possibilities of achieving economic freedom and success.

While opting for House hacking in a Family property of 1-4 units, it is possible to purchase property with less than 20% down, but it will have to be owner occupied, I.e. the owner has to reside in one of the vacant units of the house while renting other units out. With this in mind, getting an FHA loan for this unit (2-4) is possible with a 3.5% down payment. This loan gotten from FHA is called 203b, and it allows you to purchase 1-4 units dwelling houses.

However with 5+ loan, lenders usually looks at the ability of the buildings to pay for itself. If the rental property income does not meet the payments fee, insurance and taxes plus vacancy factor, they are likely not to grant such a property loan access, as they prefer down payments of more than the usual twenty-one percent.

Chapter 5
Large Apartment Complexes

Apartment complexes

The past instances low-interest fees, which started with the turn of the millennium, at first, it reduced the demand for apartments. This was because many prospective renters were in a position to buy housing, because of the decline in interest rates translated to a lower primary monthly and interest cost.

Notwithstanding, this extra demand for single-family housing quickly translated itself into a lot of expensive houses. Amazingly, this increase in price on housing has created a similar higher demand for rental units.

This is because the result of higher housing fees was to buy off potential customers out of the housing market, even after being helped through the decrease in interest rates. Due to this, they could not manage to buy a home, and so became compelled to patronize rental markets, creating an increase in the price of rent, in the short run, supply for both apartments and residential housing became insensitive to cost; due to the time needed to get planning approval, building permits and of cause construction.

On the long run, the supply of apartments remains inelastic because authorities often discourage the development of flats due to fears of excessive demands on schools, roads, and other municipal services.

Investing in apartments typically produces better returns and much less risk than investing in a residential real estate. This is because residences are less expensive to build, operate, and maintain on a per unit base. Similarly, apartments do not get stuck up in the amenity value problems that signifies single-family homes.

Apartments are purchased and sold strictly on their monetary cost and value, that is, determined by their ability to produce a net cash flow now and in the future. The apartment also has the advantage for investors that they do not require the personal attention of the investor.

Every area has expert rental management agencies who are very much willing to alleviate investors of their daily obligations of managing the property. Furthermore, apartments usually have sufficient economies of scale to make their cost feasible.

Commonly, apartment complexes can be classified into three sorts:

Garden *apartments,* ***Midrise*** *apartments,* and ***High-rise*** *apartments.*

Garden apartments have from one (1) to three (3) level and typically comprise of big balconies or patio areas.

Midrise apartment complexes, on the other hand, ranges from levels four (4) to level six (6). Anything higher than six levels could be classified as high-rise. Typically zoning guidelines or the price of the underlying land determines the specific kind of apartment to be built in a specific area.

An apartment complex developed downtown adjacent to a central business district is considered a *high-rise*. To amortize the excessive rate of the underlying land. Apartment complexes in suburbia are usually garden apartments because they presumably suit into their surroundings aesthetically and to make fewer needs on municipal services. That is probably to be enforced by zoning legal guidelines even where there may be a financial incentive to build *midrise* or *high-rise* complexes. As a general rule, the price of building apartment units rises greater than proportionately as height rises.

The demand for apartments of every type grows a long time in our society. Circular variations in apartment request do occur. However, strong long-term fundamentals in this market seek to label apartments an excellent form of investment opportunity regarding the risk-return yields. This growth is defined by an increasing population of immigrants, the lifestyles cycle of young adults leaving home and renting before they are equipped for the responsibilities of possessing a home. The supply of housing apartments is pretty inelastic within the short term (something under one year), however more elastic (sensitive to worth) in the long term (that period it takes to develop new apartment properties and convey them to the market).

The combination of inelastic short-run supply and much elastic long-run supply can create the "boom" and "bust" cycle that occasionally occurs in business buildings and shopping centers. What happens based on this is that where the call for apartments exceeds the supply, then the rents begin to rise dramatically. This rise in rentals makes it worthwhile for real investors and developers continue to bring on a unit on the market.

Since numerous investors and developers make this selection independently, there's a bent for so many units to arrive concurrently on the market that makes supply suddenly exceeds demand and rentals fall precipitously. While this cyclical effect for apartments is not well known as that of office buildings and shopping centers, this effect exists. In as much as long as the investor is conscious of the existence of this cycle, it could be used to pick out appropriate opportunities for significant profits. Buying while rents are down can be a grand thing (as long as falling rents do not pose problems such as a decline in the neighborhood of the rented apartment or a drop in the financial base of such area) and marketing when rents are high is also a good thing.

Investors in apartments also enjoy the advantages of being informed about the existence of a precise index of excess demand or excess supply. This index is the vacancy price-worth in apartments(an easily obtainable, domestically publicized figure). Where the applicable vacancy price-worth is above 20%, there may be a massive supply of apartments within the market and rents will be heading down. While the vacancy price is below 5%, then one can boldly hope towards speedy rising rents.

There is a significant caveat to note. The vacancy price rate should always be relevant to the particular market the apartment property under consideration serves. It could be that the citywide vacancy price rate is 25%, signaling an overbuilt state of affairs. However, if the apartment considered for rental approval is found on the suburban fringe; in a well-desired location and has a rapidly spread out population, then that 25% vacancy price rate might not be relevant to that precise apartment.

A beautiful approach to developing apartments in recent years has engaged conversions of properties designed for other functions to apartments(or condos). School buildings, factories, office construction, storage warehouse, and department stores have all been converted advantageously into rental apartments. This is because these properties were obtainable for a low value, having been depreciated while their historical purposes become outdated. Furthermore, these facilities were discovered in an area that befits apartment dwellers. All that made it possible to turn such property into successful investments supply.

Types of Apartment

i. Studio apartment

The smallest self-contained flats are known as studio, efficiency or bachelor flats in the U.S, or studio flat in the united kingdom. These units usually encompass a large single main room which acts as the living room, dining room and bedroom combined and usually includes kitchen facilities, with a separate smaller bathroom.

A bedsit is a United Kingdom variation on single room accommodation which makes use of bathroom facilities shared with other bedsits.

Moving up from those smaller devices are one-bedroom residences, in which a bedroom is separate from the rest of the bedroom apartment, followed by 2-bedroom, 3-bedroom, and many others. Apartments (apartments that contains more than three bedrooms are rare in rental markets). Small flats often have only one entrance.

Large apartments often possess two (2) entrances, perhaps a door in the front yard and backyard, or from an underground or otherwise connected parking structure. Dependent on the building design, the entrance doors may be attached directly outside or to an unusual area inside, such as a hallway or a lobby.

ii. Garden Apartment

The terminology 'garden' apartment is variously described, following different regional practices.

In some locales, a garden apartment complex consists of magnet rise apartment buildings constructed with landscaped grounds surrounding them. The apartment buildings often organized around courtyards that are open at one stop. Any such garden apartment shares its characteristics with a townhouse: every apartment has its very own entrance or shares that entrance through a staircase and foyer that adjoins different units above and below it. Unlike a townhouse, each condo occupies only one level. Such garden apartment homes are often not higher than three stories because they are without lack elevators/lifts. However, the primary "lawn rental" buildings in New York, United States of America, constructed in the early 1900s, was five stories high.

In other locales, a garden apartment is a unit built at or beneath grade. The name implies garden residences have direct view a garden from the unit, which is not always the case.

In almost all American west coast towns, the need for resisting earthquakes at a low building cost price results in the creation of many low-rise apartments of wood frames with skinny plaster-board based exterior and dry interior walls, notwithstanding occasionally being on as many as three or 4 levels

iii. Secondary suite

When part of a building is reconstructed for the likely use of a landlord's family member, the unit can be referred to as an in-law apartment or granny flat, though those (often illegally) created ordinary renters often occupy units as opposed to family members. In Canada, these suites are usually positioned in house basements and are often referred to as basement suites or "mother-in-law suites."

iv. Maisonette

Maisonette (from the French word maisonnette, which means "little house") can be used to differentiate dwellings that have their entrance independent from the rest of a multi-story block. This is more different to flats, which can be reached through shared entrance doors, stairs or corridors.

v. Two-story flat

In Milwaukee vernacular structure, a polish flat is a small cottage or house that has been lifted up to cater the creation of a new basement floor housing a separate apartment, then set down again; as a consequence turning into a modest two-story flat.

Most apartments are along one level, which is why they are regarded as a "flat." An apartment on more than one level, owning to itself an internal staircase which can also be referred to as a "duplex."

vi. Loft apartment

Loft apartments are often constructed from former commercial homes. while industrial traits are developed into condominiums as opposed to residences, they may be referred to as loft condominiums.

The general period warehouse-to-loft conversions may additionally once in a while be used for development of business homes into apartments and condos. "loft-fashion" may also refer definitely to developments in which a road-level commercial enterprise occupies the first ground at the same time as rental "lofts" are located above the primary ground

vii. Communal apartment

A communal rental is usually shared among several households. every family has their room, which served as a dwelling room, eating room, and bedroom for the entire family. The hallways, kitchen, bathroom, and cellphone are shared among all the residents. the communal condo turned into the essential form of housing within the united states of America for generations, and nevertheless, exist in "the most fashionable important districts of massive Russian cities."

viii. Serviced Apartment

A serviced apartment (also known as a provider rental or a prolonged stay condominium) is a supplied condo available for quick-term or lengthy-term life, presenting inn-like facilities which include room carrier, a gym, a laundry room, and a rec room. Maximum of them are prepared with complete kitchens, Wi-Fi and in-rental washers and dryers.

ix. And others.

Classes of Property

Why the classification of properties is vital?

- True benchmarking

- permits an owner to pinpoint unique marketplace strengths

- shows property's relative funding grade over the years

- more correct forecasts that are particular to property-class

- better improvement website online choice

Moreover, real classification becomes extra powerful with GIS overlays with metrics like household income, capital markets facts, employment increase and others. This adds any other layer of actionable choices.

Investors, creditors, and brokers have evolved multifamily investment property classifications to make it less difficult to speak among themselves just about investment properties and areas. The general property classifications used are A, B, C, and D.

These letter grades are allotted to properties and areas by characteristics consisting of age, tenant income level, growth areas, appreciation, facilities/amenities, and apartment charges, to name a few. It is vital to recognize property class and area class before investing so you get, the picture on how they can affect your investments, and so you can meet and surpass your investment goals and desires.

"Class A" properties are newer homes constructed inside the last 15 years including more facilities, highest income earning tenants, lowest vacancies, and could call for the highest rents with no deferred maintenance. Institutional investors are usually owners of these properties. These property demand the lowest capitalization rates (4-6%), highest per unit charges, and typically possess maximum appreciation capacity, however lowest cash flow starting out.

"Class B" properties encompass properties built in the last 15-30 years with few facilities; rents can be a bit lower than that of Class A properties with low deferred upkeep. These property demands rent slightly lower than that of Class A buildings, with a combination of white-collar employees and more professional blue collar employees.

Class B properties are usually owned by using institutional traders and private investment agencies, or by individuals with very high net worth income. They may be worth slightly higher CAP charges than Class A buildings and usually have appreciation capacity with decent cash flow on the purchase.

"Class C" properties are usually older properties, constructed 30+ years ago with tons fewer amenities than Class B if any; rents are respectively lower than Class B homes and typically have deferred maintenance and a decrease occupancy rate.

Your tenant base can be primarily blue-collar service personnel and may have a combination of government-subsidized tenants. These properties are owned by private traders/investors and private investment corporations, and also offer for higher cash flow and CAP charges, however with lower appreciation.

"Class D" properties are ancient properties in dangerous regions coupled with challenging neighborhoods. They are older, without any facility of any sort, they have high deferred maintenance and protection, functional obsolescence, and the tenant base can be very hard and mostly management intensive. These homes usually have double-digit CAP charges and most times excludes appreciation potential. Class D buildings are most challenging and do not advocate for investors, Even new investors/traders. While they might seem like Cash flow kings, the cash flow is frequently wasted, due to repairs and inability of tenants to pay their rents.

The Retired Landlord

Chapter 6
Finding an Agent

Before making your home available on the market or starting up to shop for a new one, there is a need for you to identify a real estate agents in your community who can help with the sale. Over the globe, more than two million people possess licenses to sell a real estate property, and it is their job to be an expert at the properties in their network.

They track real estate trends and are always in the business of serving people in the areas of buying and selling homes. In case you are in the market for a new home or property, it is wise to understand ways to discovering a real estate agent.

Whether you are a first-time dealer or someone who is on the lookout looking to purchasing his/her first home, there are several methods to discover a real estate agent:

Locating an excellent real property agent/broker is vital to enjoying a painless real estate transaction. The adage that

"20% of the sellers do 80% of the business," and it is very accurate. The query is how do you find a real estate agent? The great agent for you does not necessarily have to work at the most significant brokerage, close the most transactions or make the most money. The best agent for you is an experienced expert who will always listen to you, ethically conduct him /herself and knows your class.

How to find a real estate agent

1. Use the *"Find a Realtor"* tool on realtor.com to find individuals who market real estate property.

2. Referrals

Most of all the real estate agents remain in business due to the satisfaction they provide their clients. This satisfaction allows friends, family, neighbors, and coworkers to refer real estate agents business. Successful agents map their number one priority to meeting their customer's satisfaction.

3. Attend Open Houses

Going to open houses sometimes present to the opportunity of meeting real agent outside working environment. These opportunities enable you even to collect business cards.

4. *Track Neighborhood Signs*

It pays to be vigilant to notice boards in your neighborhood. Make a note of how these signposts go up and disappear. It is essential that you do not wait for a sold sign because not all agents buy the idea of posting a sold sign. However, take note that the who sells listing faster is better than an agent who has a significant number of properties on "for sale." Results speak better than volumes.

5. Using Print Advertising

Real estate Agents advertises real estate for two purposes. One is to sell specific real estate while the other is to promote their real estate agency, I.e., to promote their work.

6. Recommendations from Professionals

Real estate agents tend to refer clients to other agents. In fact, they are always happy to refer buyers and sellers to associates once they discover that the services need of such client is not their area of specialization. Some agents tend to specialize in residential resale, others on commercial or investment property, while some prefer working with new homes builders.

Questions to ask a real estate agent

i. What services do you provide?

What form of illustration do you offer? There are numerous forms of representation in.

ii. What experience do you have in my residing area?

iii. How long are homes in this neighborhood usually vacant and available on the market? ·

iv. How do you value my house?

v. How will you market my home?

vi. What is your fee?

Brokerage charges are hooked up within the marketplace and no longer set by law or regulation. The commission is the dealer's rate for managing your transaction. Ask if there are other expenses you'll pay such as an early cancellation fee, marketing fee, MLS rate or any other value that is not incorporated in the commission rate.

vii. What disclosures would you receive?

The Retired Landlord

Country rules require agents to provide vast agency disclosure information, commonly at the first a meeting with an owner or client

Chapter 7
Insurance

LLC

A *Limited Liability Company* takes responsibility for protecting personal property from allegations leveled against your company. Whenever a small business is managed without registering for any insurance, any claim that a person makes against the company also affects you individually because you are the organization. If someone accuses you and wins, you risk losing your personal properties because you haven't distinguished what belongs to the company and what belongs to you in my view. an LLC limits your legal responsibility. A claim made against the company only affects the company, not you personally.

It is an entity created under state law by filing "articles of organization" as an LLC member. Unlike sole proprietorship or partnership, none of the members of an LLC are liable for its debts. An LLC can be allotted for Federal income tax purposes as a sole proprietorship (referred to as an entity to be disregarded as separate from its owner), partnership or a corporation. If the LLC has only one owner, it will automatically be considered to be a sole proprietorship (referred to as an entity to be disregarded as separate from its owner), unless an election is established for it to be treated as a corporation.

When an LLC has two or more owners, it is considered to be partnership unless an election is decreed for it to be treated as a corporation. If the LLC does not elect its classification, a default classification of partnership (multi-member LLC) or sole proprietorship (single member LLC) will apply."

Advantages of LLC

1. Limited Liability

As the name implies, members' liabilities for the debts and obligations of the LLC are restricted to their investment. This is one of the significant advantages of a constrained liability business enterprise. If your business enterprise gets sued, your private properties, like bank account and real estate property, are protected. In most cases, one is only permitted to lose the money you put into the business, nothing more.

Keep in mind that this protection isn't always all-encompassing. Participants can nevertheless be held liable for crook conducts or if they neglect to comply with definite rules approximately enterprise management. Talk over with a lawyer to ensure you aren't violating these guidelines and exposing your self to personal legal responsibility.

2. **Pass through taxation:**

For taxation purposes, earnings from your enterprise can be handled as personal profits and are therefore not subjected to federal taxes for which corporations are responsible for.

3. **Limitless Ownership**

A few legal structures limit the number of people allowed to file as proprietors. With LLC, there is no limit to the number of owners. An LLC could decide to have one member or hundreds of individuals.

4. **Allocation Flexibility**

In an LLC, the quantity of money that owners invest into the commercial enterprise does not have to be equal to their ownership percentages. While an LLC is formed, individual members create an operating agreement, in which distinct rates of business enterprise profits and losses may be assigned to proprietors no matter the quantities of their initial investments.

5. Freedom of Management

In contrast to standard corporations, LLCs are not required to have a board of directors, annual meetings, or strict book requirements. This can free up loads of time and stress to permit you to run your business according to your terms. As you could believe, this can be a crucial advantage added to Limited Liability Company too.

Disadvantages of LLC

1. Building Capital

Unlike corporations, which issue stock to increase companies funds, LLCs need to work a bit harder to find investors and sources of capital due to the extra-legal duties and state filings involved to adding members to LLC.

2. Higher Fees

LLCs, pay extra costs to document as LLCs in comparison to a few different enterprise entities or sole proprietorships. Moreover, many states require yearly renewal charges.

3. Government Regulation

Due to protections afforded to LLCs, some types of businesses are ineligible to document as LLCs. Banks, insurance organizations, and medical service provider agencies are examples of companies that can be barred from filing in a particular state.

4. Lack of case law

The LLC enterprise form is a relatively new idea. As a result, not all cases have been determined to surround LLCs. Case law is essential due to predictability.

5. Taxation

Even though LLCs permit proprietors to keep away from federal taxes, your organization might end up paying more than it should with a different model, relying upon your state's income tax requirements, and the attribute of the enterprise. Operating with an accountant and tax attorney is an appropriate manner while planning your enterprise and forming your LLC.

6. Confusion across states

The regulations concerning LLCs range from nation to nation. If you decide to begin doing enterprise in multiple states, it may end up problematic to understand and abide by all the necessities of each country, and in a few cases, it may be necessary to form subsidiary entities to operate in different countries.

Umbrella insurance

This is mostly considered a secondary or additional liability insurance. This type of insurance policy is configured to help protect from significant claims and lawsuits. As a result, it helps protect your business and future. This kind of protection is performed in two ways: first by providing additional liability coverage above homeowners, auto or any subscribed insurance policy. This kind of insurance kicks in when primary liabilities on these other policies have been exhausted. And secondly, it provides insurance on excluded claims such as false arrest, slander, and others.

Umbrella insurance policy provides coverage for injuries, damage to property, certain lawsuits, and personal liability situations.

Types of coverage provided by an umbrella policy

1. Bodily Injury Liability

2. Property Damage Liability

3. Owners of Rental Units

Remember there is also coverage on Slander, Libel, False arrest, detention, or imprisonment, malicious prosecution, shock/mental anguish and other personal liability situations.

Advantages of an Umbrella policy

I. Better legal responsibility limits on top of both homeowners and vehicle policies. Umbrella coverage can be valuable in case of a catastrophic loss, consisting of one or more deaths or life-changing injuries. Limits of $one million to $5,000,000 are readily available for a minimum price.

Ii. A few insurers will increase the bounds for injuries to you and your circle of relatives as much as the umbrella limits.

Iii. Lots more safety of your property and future earnings, and enhanced potential to avoid embarrassing financial disaster complaints that can be required when you have low coverage for a catastrophic loss.

Iv. Better coverage (many more claims/court cases protection). It encompasses claims for libel and slander. Even if there is a dispute about whether or not the lawsuit is covered, the policy may additionally contribute drastically to a settlement, making more money (from coverage agencies) potentially available to lure the claimant/plaintiff into settling without the risk and inconvenience of a trial.

V. Supposing there is a dispute about whether the claim/lawsuit is included in the insurance, the policy may additionally make substantial contributions to a settlement, thereby creating extra cash (from coverage corporations) available to lure the claimant/plaintiff into settling without the danger and inconvenience of a trial.

Vi. Some another benefit few people are aware of is that the umbrella coverage typically may be endorsed to provide uninsured and under-insured motorist insurance to you in the amount of the umbrella coverage.

Disadvantages of umbrella policy

I. The cost and ease of implementation are the two most prominent disadvantages of an umbrella policy. The regulations aren't precisely cheap (standard range is $500 to $1,500 per $1m of coverage, depending on the risk), and the umbrella provider must pre-approve the policies it's going to provide the umbrella over.

Ii. The coverage effective dates may need to be realigned and. An umbrella carrier requires all of the underlying rules to have extreme limits of insurance. Each of those requirements makes it hard to feature an umbrella coverage.

Iii. The usually understood gain of umbrella coverage is that for a minimum value you get additional protection towards losses because of your negligence. What many don't know is that the duty to defend also exists on an umbrella policy, so attorneys to justify a claim against you will also be paid by the insurance company.

Iv. Risks to umbrella regulations are thin. In theory, someone might be more willing to pursue a claim if they recognize you have got extra coverage insurance. That's mostly a non-issue due to the fact you would by no means need to discuss policy limits with a claimant in the first place. If someone thinks they have a claim against you, you tender that claim to your coverage company and leave the conversation to them. Price rarely qualifies as a downside.

Chapter 8
Tax Benefits

Tax policy has three major purposes:

(1) To elevate revenue

(2) To gain the social end of greater income equality, and

(3) To foster befitting financial policies.

Tax policy has turned to be a political device, encouraged by the politics of government, which is visible in the case of depreciation (now officially referred to as "cost recovery").

If the authorities want to stimulate growth in commercial business, it will shorten the defined existence of an property class or increase the velocity in which it is depreciated so that business can accomplish a high write-off, as a result of this, business investment spending are stimulated by way of making capital investment more lucrative.

If the agenda of the day is "closing loopholes" and "taxing the wealthy," the taxing authorities will extend the existence of a property class or retard the speed at which the property depreciates. In doing this would have the effect of creating capital investment much less appealing. Unfortunately, those actions seem to be enforced in vague ways, making it more challenging to vision what has been realized via tax regulation changes.

The 'Jobs and Growth Tax Relief Reconciliation Act' of 2003 signed by President Bush into law on May 28, 2003, was an excellent example of the use of tax law as a tool of economic policy. This regulation was stretched wide and reduced the tax legal responsibility of most individuals and business groups.

Depreciation

Depreciation is a spread out expanse on an income that allows a taxpayer to regain the value or other basis of real property. It is an annual allowance for the damages and decline in quality or obsolescence of the property.

Most types of tangible property (except, land), including buildings, machinery, automobiles, furniture, and equipment are depreciable. Likewise, specific intangible property, for example, patents, copyrights, and computer software program are depreciable.

For a taxpayer to be allowed to place depreciation on an property, the property has to meet all the following necessities:

i. The property must belong to the taxpayer. Taxpayers may additionally depreciate any capital enhancements for property that he/she leases.

ii. A taxpayer must use the properties in business or an income-generating activity. If a taxpayer makes use of a property for commercial or business use and non-public purpose, the taxpayer can only effect deduction on depreciation through the commercial or business use of that property.

iii. The property needs to have a determinable useful life of more than a year.

Supposing a taxpayer meets the above requirements for a property, a taxpayer cannot be able to depreciate the following property:

a. Property positioned in service and disposed of in the same year.

b. Equipment used to create capital improvements. A taxpayer must add or allow depreciation on that equipment at the point of construction on the basis of development.

c. Certain term hobbies.

Depreciation starts while a taxpayer places the property in service to be used in a trade or business or for the creation of profits. The property ceases to be depreciable while the taxpayer has recovered the properties' value or other basis or while the taxpayer retires it from service, whichever happens first.

A taxpayer must identify numerous objects to ensure the right depreciation of belonging, together with:

i. The depreciation technique for the property

ii. The class life of the property

iii. Whether the properties are "listed properties."

iv. Whether or not the taxpayer elects to expense any portion of the property

v. Whether or not the taxpayer qualifies for any "bonus" first-year depreciation

vi. The depreciable foundation of the property

The Modified Accelerated Cost Recovery System (MACRS) is the right depreciation approach for most property.

Depreciation represents a tax guard for sales. Current tax coverage adjustments have shifted the amount of depreciation that may be billed to the life of the capital property to a shorter period and "the front-loaded." the quantity that can be depreciated in a given 12 months. Both of those adjustments make real estate investment extra appealing. The aggressive nature of the real estate funding system can place stress on profit margins. The tax benefits derived from depreciation could make the difference between mediocre final results and an incredible final results for the real estate investor.

Write-off

A write-off is a reduction in the income price of earning by the amount of an expense or loss. While businesses document their profits tax return, they can be capable of writing off charges incurred to run the business and subtract them from their revenue to determine their taxable profits. For instance, should in case you spend money on dinner to take out a customer/client, a part of that expense acts as a write-off in opposition to your commercial business income because the price of the dinner is a business-associated expense.

Likewise, imagine one of your clients in business owes you money, but the business of that clients has been declared bankrupt and is not able to pay the invoice to your company. The bad debt is considered a loss your accountant can write off on your tax return. A write-off is a sort of deduction, and in some cases, the words can be applied interchangeably. For example, while a self-employed individual or small commercial enterprise owner document his income tax return, he regularly refers to his business write-offs as a deductions/reduction.

For instance, a write off is remitted when an account receivable cannot be raised, while inventory is obsolete, while there may be no use for a fixed property, or when a worker leaves the organization and is not willing to pay back the advance payment rendered by his/her organization.

A write-off is achieved by transferring a few or all the balance in an property account to an expense account. The accounting can have different range, depending on the property involved.

For instance:

i. When an account receivable cannot be accumulated for, it is customarily offset against the allowance for dubious money owed (a contra account).

When a stock is obsolete, it can either be charged directly to the price of products sold or offset against the reserve for obsolete inventory (a contra account).

ii. Whilst there is no longer use for a fixed property, it is offset in opposition to all related and accumulated depreciation amortization, with the rest being charged to a loss account.

iii. When a 'pay advance' cannot be accrued for, it is then charged to compensation fee or expense.

iv. When an allowance account (contra account) is used, then the credit score is to an allowance account. Later, when a selected write off is observed, it is offset against such allowance account.

A write off typically occurs immediately, in place of being spread over numerous intervals, because it is triggered by a single event that is immediately recognized.

A variant on the write off idea is a write-down, in which part of the price-value of an property is charged to expense, leaving a decreased property nonetheless on the books. For instance, a settlement with a customer/client might allow for a 50% reduction in the amount charged that the customer/client will pay. This represents a write-down on one-half of the amount of the original cost.

Management from time to time speed up the use of write-downs and write-offs to recognize expenses and thereby reduce the number of taxable earnings. While taken to an extreme point, this will bring about fraudulent financial statements.

Negative write-offs

A negative write-off is mostly the opposite of a typical write-off in that it refers to a business enterprise conclusion to no-longer payback or settle the account of a person or business enterprise that has overpaid.

The use of the situation above, if a client can pay the complete fee for a product on credit terms, and then after the payment is made, the same client was allowed to realize a discount, it lies on the company to decide to credit back the discounted amount to such client. If the companies decision is to keep the payment and not credit the amount of discount, it is then considered to be a negative write-off.

Negative write-offs can damage relationships with clients and can also cause adverse legal implications.

How tax write-offs work

Tax-write offs simply decrease an 'individual or business' taxable income and for this reason the tax liability. For example, imagine your business enterprise earns $100,000 in sales, however, spends $50,000 on payroll, utilities, lease/rents, stock and other operating expenses. When you report your earnings tax return, you file the income and the cost-expenses, and due to the write-offs, your taxable business earnings is only $50,000.

WRITE-OFFS VS. CREDIT

Credits are sometimes mixed-up with deductions and write-offs, and despite the fact that they decrease your tax liability, they work differently. A tax credit is applied to accrued tax and used to reduce it, and the refundable tax credit may even cause a tax refund. For instance, imagine you owe $10,000 in taxes, and you are eligible for a $3,000 credit. The credit brings down your tax invoice to $7,000. Further, likewise, if you owe $5,000 in taxes but qualify for a $6,000 refundable tax credit, you get hold of a $1,000 tax refund.

Conclusion

Real Estate Investment Market is quite a complex system of firms based entirely in specific sectors of the industry. The future of businesses in this sector is affected and tied to modifications in global monetary situations. Depending on what the corporation's recognition on, from land and development, apartments and multi-family homes, retail shopping centers, industry/office space, many factors are affecting their approach, overall performance, and future.

Real estate investments fall into distinctive categories. Your preference of which to invest on relies on the sort of publicity you are looking for in your portfolio. You may spend money on income-generating properties or non-profits-generating properties. Any leased/rent properties is a profit-generating property, and vacant properties are non-profits generating properties. You could earn 'capital return' on non-profits generating property, just as you will on an investment in a home.

Real estate can generate income like a bond and appreciate value like equity.

Real estate is tangible, so it requires continuous management. On the other hand, you also have an increased capableness to stimulate the performance of a single funding investment as compared to other property classes. Some of the added benefits of including real estate to a portfolio encompass Diversification, yield enhancement, reduction in risk and inflation-hedging ability. However, real estate also has excessive transaction charges, which makes it difficult to acquire, it can be challenging to measure real estate's relative performance.

Depreciation represents a tax shield for income generating revenues. Current tax coverage changes have shifted the amount of depreciation that may be charged to the existence of the capital property to a shorter period and "front-loaded" the amount that can be depreciated in a given year. Both of those modifications make real property investment extra appealing.

The principal varieties of properties for investment are offices, retails, and multi-family residential properties. The selection of an enterprise form offers exceptional possibilities for the investor to manipulate risk, maximize cash flow, and reduce taxes. At the same time, real estate business investors need to choose an insurance coverage scheme, be it Limited Liability Company (LLC) or any other coverage scheme.

There is enough money to be made in real estate, with buying at market value and making profits over a long haul or purchasing below the market for a quick turnaround (flipping).

www.ingramcontent.com/pod-product-compliance
Lightning Source LLC
Chambersburg PA
CBHW052301220526
45471CB00001B/441